CIVILIZATION IN BRITAIN

The Myth Of The Megalithic Builders Revealed

T.F.G. Dexter

OAKMAGIC PUBLICATIONS 2001

CIVILIZATION IN BRITAIN

*The Myth Of The Megalithic
Builders Revealed*

T. F. G. Dexter

*First published by Watts & Co,
1931*

This edition:

OAKMAGIC PUBLICATIONS 2001

ISBN: 1 901163 19 9

*For a list of over 80 books on all aspects
of Cornish & West Country folklore &
antiquities, send SAE to:*

*OAKMAGIC BOOKS
2 SOUTH PLACE FOLLY,
PENZANCE TR18 4JB*

or visit our website at:

www.oakmagicpublications.com

EPITOME

The prevalent opinion that the Britons were uncivilised (1).* Civilisation defined (2–9) : also History, Archæology, and Stone, Bronze and Iron Ages (10). Artifacts (coins, enamels, etc.) of Early Iron Age *prove* civilisation of some Britons (11–14), an opinion confirmed by the Classics (15). Reasons for idea that Britons were savages (16). Parts of Britain civilised in Early Bronze Age and perhaps in Late Stone Age (17–23). How Britain lost this archaic civilisation (24) which was derived from the East (25), an opinion supported by examination of Stonehenge (26). Megaliths—kinds, distribution, and probable origin (27–29). The possibility of an ancient, wondrous civilisation which may have originated in Egypt and diffused itself over the then known world (30–33). Spain, a clearing-house between East and West (34). The Egyptians skilful sailors (25–40). Indications that they came to Britain (41–47), seeking gold and pearls—a religious quest (48–55). Tin valued for utilitarian purposes as a constituent of bronze (56–60). The conjunction of megaliths with gold, pearls, jet (sacred); tin, flint, copper, lead, hæmatite (useful) (61–65). The theory " metals and megaliths " holds good nearly everywhere (66–72). Egyptians were colonists and influenced the aborigines profoundly (73–77), as seen in the " Spaniards," really " Egyptians," in Cornwall and elsewhere to-day (78). Influence of " Egyptians," even if only transient visitors, would be great (79). Conclusion. Our History should begin not with Cæsar's Invasion, 55 B.C., but with the building of Avebury, cir. 2000 B.C. (80, 81).

* The numbers refer to sections, not pages.

LIST OF ILLUSTRATIONS

CIVILISATION IN BRITAIN
2000 B.C.

1. ALONG the Malabar Coast in Southern India are to be found fairly large communities of native Christians who do not owe their Christianity to any comparatively recent attempts to convert India. These native Christians maintain that their ancestors were converted by St. Thomas the Apostle in the first century. That may or may not be, but one thing is fairly certain : they have been Christians from a very early date, perhaps as early as the sixth century.

A fussy wife of a newly-appointed Anglo-Indian Official went into one of the schools of these native Christians, and going up to the Master, asked in a rather supercilious way : " My dear man, when were you converted to Christianity ? " " Madam," he answered, " my ancestors were Christians when yours were heathen savages who went about half-naked, painted in woad." " Savages," " half-naked," " painted in woad " ! This Hindu was repeating only what the English had taught him, for this idea is a current one among us to-day.

2. A few years ago, so-called comic artists were fond of depicting half-clad Ancient Britons with negroid features fleeing in terror from gigantic " crocodiles " and other awesome beasts. Most of us are old enough to recollect these pictures, which, fortunately for the truth, seem to be now out of fashion. These drawings had many anachronisms, but two only need be mentioned—the fearsome reptiles depicted were extinct long before man appeared on the earth, and the Ancient Britons (and by Ancient Britons we mean those peoples who so valiantly opposed the Romans) were, as we shall see, civilised, and here it may be well to make a digression and endeavour to explain what is meant by civilisation.

3. It is fairly easy to say that such and such a tribe or people is savage, semi-civilised or civilised, but it is not easy

to define the term *civilisation* itself.   The word *civil* in civilisation is connected with the Latin word *civis*, " citizen," and with our English word *civility*, which nowadays means " politeness," but which once upon a time signified " the state or condition of being a citizen."   So there would seem to be some connection between civilisation and being a citizen, and philology apparently indicates that men became civilised when they commenced to live in cities, and when they learned to be civil or polite to one another.

4. As long as men lived in families and considered only members of their own family, there was really no civilisation, but when many families commenced to live together in communities (villages, towns, cities), and when men began to learn to be civil or polite to people outside their own families, then civilisation began.   Now some men are nature's gentlemen, they are naturally considerate of others.   But, unfortunately, there are some who are bullies; others, grasping and greedy; and yet others, rascals in one way or another.   So rules or laws gradually arose telling these bullies and rascals how they were to behave and punishing them if they behaved badly.   And thus we find the presence of rules or laws another sign of civilisation.

5. When men began to live together in communities, it was soon found that some could do certain things much better than others.   Accordingly, the men clever in making things out of wood became the carpenters; those expert in working iron, the blacksmiths; and so on.   Again, some men showed themselves adepts in buying and selling goods, and in speaking the languages of other peoples, and thus arose the merchant class.   This process is sometimes described as a differentiation of function.

6. But in a really stable state, these classes must not be totally segregated from one another; they must retain the capacity of combination for the common good and the common safety.

7. So we may now enumerate a few of the chief signs of civilisation :—

(a) Living together in large communities—villages, towns, cities—as citizens.

(b) Among these citizens the reign of law protecting the weak against the strong.

(c) The classification of these citizens according to the work they could do best, that is, differentiation of function, and lastly,

(d) A capacity of combination among the various classes of citizens.

8. We are too apt to think that civilisation means printing, elaborate machinery, science, etc., but some of these things sometimes tend rather to destroy than to promote real civilisation. Thus, printing brings with it " snippet " literature, which discourages prolonged continuity of thought; machinery is apt to make the man who tends it into a machine; the blessings of science bring with them poison gas and the Zeppelin !

9. The opinion of a few scientists notwithstanding, there would really seem to be a rough-and-ready correspondence between the size of the head and mental capacity. Leaving aside abnormal cases, such as water-on-the-brain, we find that, generally speaking, the larger the head, the greater the intelligence. Anthropologists are often puzzled because the cranial capacity of ancient man is sometimes greater than that of some of the inhabitants of our crowded cities to-day. The reason is not far to seek. Man of old had to think how to provide his wife, his children and himself with food, shelter and clothing. He *had* to think or perish. Many modern men do not have to think. The State does all the thinking for them.

The man who three thousand years ago shot birds with bow and arrow for food may have been more intelligent and quite as civilised as the modern man who shoots them with a gun for sport.

10. But before we can proceed far with our investigations, there are other terms which require elucidation, and among them History and Archæology.

By History is generally understood a knowledge of past events gleaned from written records, and written records regarding Britain are very few previous to Julius Cæsar's invasions in the middle of the first century before Christ. If we wish to learn much before that time, we have to study what are sometimes called prehistoric monuments, such as

Stonehenge, and the cromlechs, barrows and hill-camps which dot our landscapes : also the artifacts or works of men, which the spade from time to time reveals to us. This study is known as Archæology, a word meaning a knowledge of ancient things.

The Archæologist divides the ancient history of man into three great stages :—

    (1) THE STONE AGE (from the earliest times to about 1800 B.C.), when man used knives, weapons and other

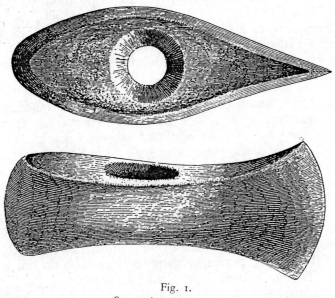

Fig. 1.
STONE AXE HAMMER.

implements made of stone. The Neolithic or New Stone Age is the later and the more important period of this era.

    (2) THE BRONZE AGE (from about 1800 B.C. to 450 or 300 B.C.), when he used implements made of bronze, an alloy or mixture of copper and tin in the proportions of about nine parts of copper to one of tin. (Fig. 2.)

    (3) THE IRON AGE (from about 450 or 300 B.C.), when he became acquainted with the use of iron, and developed its use to the present day, which may be described as the Age of Machinery.

This tri-partite division was first formulated by Sir John Lubbock (afterwards Lord Avebury), and at the time the division seemed a good one, but fuller knowledge has shown it to be not entirely satisfactory. Still, this division has to stand because we cannot as yet find anything better.

11. An endeavour will now be made—

(i) To prove that some at any rate of the Ancient Britons at the time of the Roman Invasions were civilised, and,

(ii) To establish a strong presumption that there was a civilisation in parts of these Islands as early as the beginning of the Bronze Age, *cir.* 1800 B.C., or even earlier, towards the end of the Stone Age, *cir.* 2000 B.C.

Fig. 2.

BRONZE DAGGER, OF THE BRONZE AGE.

12. First, to prove that the Ancient Britons were civilised at the time of the Roman Invasions :

Many ancient British coins, mainly gold, have been found in central and southern England, and on them are engraved heads of remarkable artistic merit. (Figs. 3, 4.) As we know, the human face is a particularly difficult thing to draw, and the men who drew these heads were far removed from savages. Moreover, some counterfeit coins have been found—undoubted proofs of an advanced stage of civilisation! Competent authorities date these coins, real and counterfeit, at about 100 B.C. The queer-looking horses on the reverse are not barbaric, as is commonly supposed, but additional proofs of the civilisation of the Britons. This, how-ever, is a long story which must be deferred to a subsequent booklet.

13. Much evidence regarding the high culture of the " Ancient Britons " is furnished by the enamels found from

time to time in Britain. (Fig. 5.) Antiquaries are generally agreed that these enamels are of British manufacture, and they date them between 200 B.C. and A.D. 200. Among them we may instance that *chef-d'œuvre* of prehistoric Celtic art, the enamelled Bronze Shield found in the Thames at Battersea.

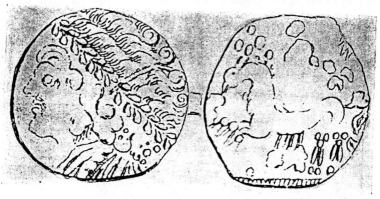

Fig. 3.

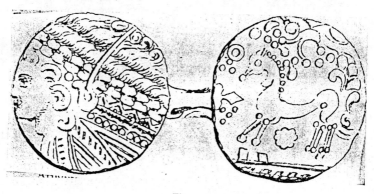

Fig. 4.
ANCIENT BRITISH GOLD COINS.
Discovered in Southern England and dated about 100 B.C.

Enamelling was unknown to the Romans until they learned it from the Celts. Philostratus, writing in the third century of our era, speaks of the Britons and their art of enamelling : "They say that the Barbarians who live in the ocean pour these colours upon heated brass, that they adhere, become hard as stone, and preserve the designs that are made upon them." The Britons were past-masters in the art of enamelling, and speaking of some enamels found in Gaul, Dr. Anderson says that these are the work of mere dabblers in the art compared with the British examples, that the home of the art was Britain, and that it had reached its highest stage of indigenous development before it came into contact with Roman culture.

The process of producing these enamels required great technical skill which meant long and laborious training on the part of the artisans, who could not have manufactured them without furnaces capable of generating a high temperature.

The existence of these art treasures implies the existence of a skilled artisan class who had spent years at their craft, the

Fig. 5.
A BRITISH ENAMEL.
From British Museum Guide to Early Iron Age.
The light parts are bright red enamel.

knowledge of which they inherited from artisans before them. It also implies a class rich enough to buy the enamels when they were made. Such artifacts betoken settled government, good laws, peace over long periods and prosperity : in short, a civilisation of no mean order.

14. Professor Haverfield is of opinion that some of the Britons knew Latin before the Christian era, and in a paper contributed to the Cambridge Antiquarian Society on the Arrentine Bowl found at Foxton, Cambridgeshire, he observes that there was " before the Claudian conquest a Celtic population prosperous enough to import and educated enough to use some of the finest products of the Continental civilisation."

15. Scattered up and down classical literature we find admissions as to the civilisation of the Britons. Posidonius,

who travelled in Britain about 90 B.C., says that " the inhabitants of Belerion (probably the Land's End) were very fond of strangers and civilised in consequence," a remark to which we shall refer again later on. Cæsar says that Britain was well peopled, full of houses, and that the Britons themselves possessed cattle in abundance—undoubted signs of civilisation. He also tells us that the Druids used Grecian letters—an indication that some British culture was of foreign origin.

More proofs of the civilisation of some of the Britons at the time of the Roman Invasions could be given, but at the

Fig. 6.
GOLD CUP, OF THE BRONZE AGE.
Found near the Cheesewring, Cornwall.

risk of wearying the reader, who will, it is hoped, agree that the question needs no further demonstration.

16. But whence arose the idea that the Britons at the era just mentioned were savages ? First, from the fact that most of the inhabitants of Northern Britain *were* at that time in a more or less savage state, only those in Central and Southern Britain being civilised. Secondly, from the fact that the Romans looked with contempt upon any civilisation different from their own, and it is mainly to the Romans that we are indebted for our accounts of Early Britain. We made exactly the same mistake when we first came into contact with the Hindus and

with the Chinese. We thought them barbarians, whereas we now know that they have a civilisation at least as old as our own, and perchance in a few respects superior.

17. Our next task is to establish a strong presumption (which it is admitted hardly yet amounts to proof) that there was a civilisation (perhaps several civilisations) in these Islands as early as the beginning of the Bronze Age, *cir.* 1800 B.C., or even earlier.

A Gold Cup, found in a round barrow near the Cheesewring in south-east Cornwall in 1837, was at the time pronounced by competent authorities to be of the Bronze Age.

Fig. 7.
THE DENZELL CUP, PROBABLY OF THE BRONZE AGE.
Found near St. Columb, Cornwall.

Unfortunately, this wondrous relic has mysteriously disappeared, but, fortunately, pictures of it are still in existence. (Fig. 6.)

A Cup very like the Cheesewring gold cup in size but beautifully carved out of a block of amber has been found near Brighton, and is pronounced by competent authorities to be of the Bronze Age. The cup found at Denzell, Mawgan in Pydar, Cornwall, seems to be modelled on the same plan as the one just mentioned, but it is made of clay, not amber. (Fig. 7.)

The gold peytrel (discovered in a barrow in Flintshire, and the ornament probably of a sacred horse) is also of the Bronze Age.

The gold Lunettes or Lunulæ found in Ireland, Cornwall, Wales and South Scotland are believed to be moon symbols.

They have well-defined and artistic ornament and are supposed to date from quite early in the Bronze Age. (Fig. 8.)

And the Gold Torques, or Torcs, so common in Ireland, are perhaps older still.

18. Stonehenge may be adduced as another indication of an early civilisation in Britain. Stonehenge was considered by Professor W. Gowland to be of rather late Neolithic Age, but Lord Avebury thought it belonged to the Bronze Period.

Fig. 8.
GOLD LUNULA, FOUND AT PAUL, CORNWALL,
and thought to be of Early Bronze Age.

Sir Norman Lockyer, working on astronomical data, arrived at a date 1680 B.C., with a possible error in either direction of two hundred years. There is now a tendency to date this megalithic monument somewhat later. The battle of the date of Stonehenge is perhaps not yet over. It is probable that, like our Cathedrals and Abbeys, different parts were erected at different times, but with this reservation, there would now seem a fair consensus of opinion among archæologists that Stonehenge was erected at the beginning of the Bronze Age, perhaps *cir.* 1800–1700 B.C.

19. Commenting on the fact that some of the stones of Stonehenge came from Pembrokeshire, Dr. R. E. M. Wheeler says : " There is no more striking fact in the whole of British pre-history than the proved transportation of the famous ' blue stones ' of Stonehenge from the mountains of Pembrokeshire to the shores of Wiltshire.   The religious and political centralisation implied by this mysterious act, in an era of forest and fen unmapped and often untracked, can scarcely have been surpassed in any later prehistoric age."   Dr. Rendel Harris thinks the stones were water-borne; first, via the Bristol Channel, and afterwards along the Avon, a far more likely hypothesis. Whichever is correct, the transport of these rock masses over such a great distance implies an intelligent direction, perhaps of slave, perchance of free labour.   In any case the feat indicates the presence of a civilisation as early as 1800–1700 B.C.

20. Avebury, perhaps originally the largest circular megalithic structure in the world, covers an area of 28½ acres and is now difficult to trace, for the village of Avebury has been built within it, largely from the stones of the circle itself. John Aubrey (1626–1697), our first real antiquary and folklorist, says that " Avebury doth as much exceed in greatness the so renowned Stonehenge as a cathedral doth a parish church," while Leslie Forbes observes that Avebury is " beyond comparison the greatest in point of extent, in the amount of labour expended, and in the size of the monoliths of which it was constructed, of any circular primitive temple as yet noticed in Asia, Africa, or Europe."   Lord Avebury, who took his title from this erst-time mighty megalith, assigned it to the end of the Stone or the beginning of the Bronze Age, probably about 2000 B.C.

Silbury Hill, the largest artificial hill in Europe, is not far away.   It covers 5½ acres, and rises to a height of 125 feet.

Nor must we omit to mention the recently discovered Woodhenge, probably older than Stonehenge, or even than Avebury itself.

21. There is yet one more indication of civilisation in the Stone Age.   Trepanning (that is, the making of an opening in the skull for relieving the brain from compression or irritation) is a surgical operation demanding no mean skill; yet in Britain skulls undoubtedly of Neolithic (Late Stone) Age have been found which show that this operation had been

performed during life with complete success. The primitive Neolithic surgeon muſt have used a sharp flint, to us a clumsy inſtrument, but flint is less likely to carry germs than ſteel— a point in which the Neolithic surgeon had an advantage over his modern representative. Yet, one cannot help marvelling that such an operation should have been possible at such an early period. The man who performed it was no savage, and we have in these trepanned skulls indications of culture in Britain in the Neolithic Age, probably 2000 years before the Chriſtian era.

22. To sum up. There are ſtrong indications (which amount nearly if not quite to proof) of a civilisation in Britain as early as 2000 or 1800 B.C. These indications become more and more certain as we descend the ages, and we may consider it *proved* that round about the time of Julius Cæsar and the birth of Chriſt Britain had a civilisation of no mean order.

23. There is little or no doubt that parts of Britain once possessed an archaic civilisation. Moſt of us have hitherto regarded Rome as a great civiliser, and it comes as somewhat of a shock to learn that some competent authorities think that Rome was largely inſtrumental in deſtroying the archaic civilisation of Britain. But this is a long tale, too long for recital here. Suffice it to say that the barbarous Saxon completely effaced the little British civilisation the Romans left.

24. An insiſtent queſtion now arises : " Whence did Britain derive this ancient civilisation ? " It is at firſt sight easy to surmise that it was derived from Greece and Rome. But Greece did not come into notice much before 1200 B.C., and the traditional date for the founding of Rome is 753 B.C. Stonehenge, built about 1800–1700 B.C., is thus more ancient than Greece and Rome, while Avebury, erected about 2000 B.C., is older ſtill. This ancient civilisation is older than the Celt in Britain. Avebury and Stonehenge were of hoary antiquity when the firſt Celt landed here about 1200 B.C. To find the sources of our moſt ancient civilisation we muſt look for something older than Greece and Rome, something older than the earlieſt of the Celts, and we are driven to look to the Eaſt, the source of moſt early culture, sacred or profane. Archæologiſts are of opinion that there was a civilisation in Egypt as early as 3500 or 4000 B.C., perhaps even as far back as 5000 B.C. The civilisation of the Babylonian area is thought by some to

be older still.   There was another primitive civilisation on the banks of the Indus.   Yet another civilisation, midway in time between the Egyptian and the Grecian, is that of Crete and the Eastern Mediterranean, *cir.* 3000 B.C.

25.   A thought : Is the source of our most ancient civilisation to be sought in Crete and the Eastern Mediterranean, or in Egypt or in Babylonia ?   Or, are its sources to be found in all three ?

Fig. 9.
A MENHIR, OR LONG STONE.

26. Both Avebury and Stonehenge are open to the sky. They have no roof and never had one.   Such buildings cannot possibly be indigenous.   No son of the soil of Britain would plan a building without some protection from the weather, and we must recollect that in 2000 B.C. there were more forests, swamps and marshes than there are now, that there was more rain, and generally speaking, the weather was probably worse than it is to-day.   No : Avebury and Stonehenge were built by men from sunnier climes, and we find ourselves driven to the East once more.

27. Having got so far we must now make a digression in order to establish the next point.   Avebury and Stonehenge

are sometimes denominated Megalithic (great-stone) Monuments, and we may roughly classify Megaliths into—

(*a*) Menhirs, Long Stones, usually upright. (Fig. 9.)

(*b*) Cromlechs (called Dolmens on the Continent), upright stones with a table-like covering-stone; probably sepulchral. (Fig. 10.)

(*c*) Circles (called Cromlechs on the Continent), probably once heathen temples. (Fig. 11.)

28. Megaliths are to be found in India, North Africa, the Black Sea coast, the Islands of the Western Mediterranean, Spain, Portugal, Brittany, North Germany, Southern Scandi-

Fig. 10.

A CROMLECH.

navia, Holland, Britain, Ireland, and going farther afield, the Isles of the Pacific and the western coast of America.

Mr. T. Eric Peet remarks that megaliths " occupy a very remarkable position along a vast seaboard which includes the Mediterranean coast of Africa and the Atlantic coast of Europe. In other words, they lie entirely along a natural sea-route."

29. Now, are we to suppose that the inhabitants of North Africa, Cornwall and Polynesia awoke one fine morning and said : " Let's build megaliths," and that they there and then proceeded to do so, and to build them all more or less alike ! The idea seems impossible, and on this point Mr. T. Eric Peet pertinently observes : " It is impossible to consider megalithic building as a mere phase through which many nations passed, and it must therefore have been a system originating with one race and spreading far and wide, owing either to trade influence or migration," while both Bertrand and Gomme think that we owe the megaliths of the world to a pre-Aryan people.

30. One thing seems to stand out as fairly certain—that long before our era there arose a powerful people (or peoples) with one of the most wonderful civilisations the world has ever seen. The members of this mighty race (or races) spread themselves and their influence far and wide, and left in many and unexpected places, grand, unmistakable and, humanly speaking, everlasting monuments of their erst-time presence.

Fig. 11.

TREGASEAL CIRCLE, CORNWALL.

(Tregaseal means "House of the Sun," and points to Sun-worship.)

31. Three questions arise :—

(i) Whence arose this wondrous race or races ?

(ii) Did they ever reach Britain ?

(iii) What impelled them to travel everywhere and to leave such mighty monuments behind them ?

We will now endeavour to answer the first question.

32. The late Dr. W. H. R. Rivers showed the close connection between the cult of the megalith and the cult of the sun. In consequence of this close connection the cult is

sometimes called heliolithic (Greek, *helios*, " sun "; *lithos*, " stone "). Dr. Rivers further hinted at Egypt as a possible place of origin. Professor Elliot Smith is more definite, for he regards ancient Egypt as the place of origin of the heliolithic peoples. By means of megalithic structures he traces the race (or races) along the northern coast of Africa, along the west of the Iberian Peninsula, through France to Brittany and thence to Britain itself. He derives the cromlech (dolmen) from the mastaba, an early form of an Egyptian tomb. This idea, like so many new ideas, has been ridiculed, and it has been objected that there are no cromlechs in Egypt, but Professor Seligman contradicts this, and states that cromlechs are to be found both in Egypt and in the Sudan. So the theory may be said to hold the field, considerable and notable opposition notwithstanding.

33. " Children of the Sun " (Dr. W. E. Perry), " Prospectors," Etruscans (Mr. H. Peake), and " Easterners " (the brothers Siret) are names variously given to these wondrous peoples, who may have been Egyptians or Babylonians or Cretans or other races from the Eastern Mediterranean, or any two or more of them. We will tentatively consider them as Egyptians and leave the possibility of Babylonian, Cretan, or other origin for a subsequent occasion.

34. Looking at a map we see that Spain is roughly halfway between Egypt and Britain. The excavations of the Sirets show that the " Easterners," as the Sirets call them, were in Spain searching for metals while the natives were still in the Stone Age, and the spades of the Sirets have been busy on the trading posts or settlements of these " Easterners " and have revealed idol-like objects made of hippopotamus ivory from Egypt, a shell found only in the Red Sea, ostrich eggs from Africa and alabaster figurines of a Babylonian type. Associated with these Oriental objects were found amber from the Baltic and jet from Britain : in short, artifacts from the East, North and West. The link between Britain on the one hand and Egypt and possibly far-off Babylon on the other would seem fairly well established; further, Spain seems to have been a sort of clearing-house between the East and the West. Still further, it seems that these " Easterners " kept the Iberian aborigines in ignorance of the use of metals. " The West was a cow to be milked, a sheep to be fleeced, a field to be cultivated, a mine to be exploited."

35. But what a long way the Egyptians had to walk to get to Britain ! Not so fast, my dear reader, not so fast. They didn't walk at all, they went by sea, and the megaliths *en route* may mark not the resting-places of pedestrians, but ports of call of early navigators.

It seems to be nearly an article of faith among some people that in ancient times long and difficult journeys were undertaken by land, not by sea. But the most ancient civilisations known were in river valleys—the Mesopotamian on the Tigris and Euphrates, the Egyptian on the Nile, the Indus civilisation in the Southern Punjab in the neighbourhood of Sindh. In a word, ancient civilisations were water-borne. Man commenced to practise navigation in the comparative safety of the quiet reaches of rivers. Only when fairly proficient did he dare the sea. When he became skilled as a seaman he seems to have found voyaging by sea really easier than journeying by land. In this connection Mr. Eric Peet says that " the sea has always been less of an obstacle to early man than the land with its deserts, mountains and unfordable rivers."

36. According to Professor Elliot Smith the art of navigation originated in Egypt. He states that practically every writer on the history of shipbuilding admits " that the evidence at our disposal points very definitely to the conclusion that naval architecture is an Egyptian art, and that the main lines of the history of shipbuilding for the whole world were laid down in Egypt towards the end of the fourth millennium B.C." In support of this idea we may note the definite record that Seneferu, the last king of the third dynasty (*cir.* 3100 B.C.), built a fleet of 40 ships, each 150 feet in length, which sailed to Syria and brought away cedar-wood for his palace, an undoubted reference to a sea-voyage at an early date.

37. One of the few secular tales of Egypt that have come down to us is called *The Castaway*, and was written probably in the third millennium B.C. The Castaway narrates that he set out for the Mines of Honham and went to sea in a ship, 150 cubits long and 40 cubits wide (about 225 feet and 60 feet respectively), with 150 of the best sailors in the land of Egypt. The ship foundered, and the Narrator, the only survivor, was cast upon an island, where he found a new ship, fully manned, in which he reached Egypt after a voyage of two months.

Two things in this account are very significant—the

voyage was to some mines (the situation of which is unknown), and these mines were more than two months' sail from Egypt, for the implication is that the Castaway was wrecked before he reached them.   Pliny speaks of the Egyptians visiting Taprobane (*hodie*, Ceylon), and the tale just narrated tells us that they made long and difficult voyages in search of metals.

38. The earliest known representation of a sea-going ship was found in the tomb of the Egyptian king, Sahure, of the fifth dynasty, *cir.* 2600 B.C.   A boat of Mediterranean type, 42 feet long and dated before 1100 B.C., has been found near the Clyde, embedded in silt, and 25 feet above present sea-level.   It has a plug of cork which could have come only from the area where cork trees grow—Spain, South France and Italy—but whether this boat came from Egypt or not is uncertain.

39. Perchance the influence of the nautical skill of the Egyptians lasted down to the time of Julius Cæsar, who paid a high tribute to the sailor-like qualities of the Veneti in Brittany, for he admitted that their ships were vastly superior to his own, and so strong that they easily withstood the impact of the Roman vessels when the latter tried to ram them.   Brittany is a metalliferous area, just one of the places the ancient Egyptians may have exploited.   It is also megalithic.   Carnac in Brittany is one of the megalithic wonders of the world.   Twelve hundred rough columnar stones, 5 to 20 feet high, still remain. Was Carnac built by the Egyptians, and did the Veneti learn the art of navigation from them?   The Britons helped the Veneti against the Romans, and we may be sure they were no mean allies.   Perhaps they derived their skill from the same source.   An Egyptian version of " Britannia rules the Waves " might have been first sung on the Mediterranean, just outside the delta of the Nile, by those daring Egyptian navigators who first essayed and conquered the vasty deep.

40. Sir Arthur Keith in his Presidential Address to the Students' Scientific Society, Aberystwyth, in October 1928, said that Professor Fleure and himself were of opinion that during the second millennium B.C. ships were entering St. George's Channel " carrying new men, new beliefs, new customs and new arts.   We now realised that the lane which ended at our western portal began in the distant East—the cradle of modern civilisation.   Thus did these ancient Mediterranean sea-dogs, by an early exercise of sea-power, obtain dominion

in Western Britain." As we have already observed, the ocean path of these peoples may be traced by cromlechs and other megaliths from the African coast through Spain and Brittany to Cornwall, to the west of Wales and to the east of Ireland.

41. We will now consider the indications (which as yet hardly amount to proof) that the ancient Egyptians came to Britain.

Stonehenge is in Wiltshire, and in the early Bronze Age barrows of that county have been found many blue glass beads of peculiar shape and hue. Both Professor Sayce of Oxford and Dr. H. R. Hall of the British Museum identify these beads as Egyptian, and date them about 1500–1300 B.C. So there would appear to be indications of Egyptian influence, if not indeed of the presence of Egyptians, in the neighbourhood of Stonehenge in the middle of the second millennium before our era. But we must bear in mind the caveat issued by Sir Arthur Evans, that "the possibility cannot be altogether excluded that some of the Faience beads found in the British Isles are of local fabric."

42. Professor Elliot Smith compares some early skeletons found in British barrows with those found in Somaliland. And in this connection it should be noted that Professor Sayce compares the natives of Kerry with the Berbers of North Africa.

43. Sir J. Morris Jones considers that non-Aryan traits of syntax found in Celtic tongues point unmistakably to old Egyptian and Berber and to other idioms of the Southern Mediterranean.

44. In Cornwall are found peculiarly carved menhirs with a stone circle (more often than not pierced with holes) above, standing on a stone slab or "collar," with a long cone-like shaft below. (Fig. 12.) An extreme example is to be seen in Camborne churchyard, where the girth of one of the "crosses" under the collar is 3′ 3″, and on the ground level 6′ 8″. These menhirs are popularly called "crosses," but they are no more like true Christian crosses than chalk is like cheese. They bear, however, a strong resemblance to Egyptian ankhs (Fig. 13), which as depicted in the hands of Egyptian gods have not only handles and collars but cone-like shafts. They seem to suggest Egyptian influence, and the full story of the influence of the Egyptian ankh upon Christian symbolism has yet to be written.

45. The practice of dropping pins into holy wells is well known and not yet obsolete. But in some parts of Cornwall, and perhaps elsewhere, the pin, to be efficacious, must be a bent one. There is no doubt that the dropping of a pin into a well is of heathen origin : there is nothing Christian about it. No one has apparently supplied an explanation of the reason the pin must be bent. May I hazard one ? The Egyptian hieroglyph for an offering to a god is a bent piece of wire; so the bent pin may be a folk memory of a pagan offering to the divinity of the well. If this explanation be correct, we have here yet one more link with Egypt.

Fig. 12.

Composite Picture
of
CORNISH ROUND-HEADED
" CROSS " (so called).

Fig. 13.

EGYPTIAN ANKH.
" Symbol of Life."

Found in hands of
Egyptian Gods.

46. Dr. Rendel Harris, in the *Woodbrooke Essays*, has shown the probability that some place-names which elude the Celtic and the Teutonic philologist fall an easy prey once the possibility of an Egyptian origin is admitted.

There are other indications—not proofs—of Egyptian influence in Britain, but space forbids their elaboration. It looks as though the evidence is cumulative, and that in time the presence of Egyptians in early Britain will be accepted as an undoubted fact.

47. We will now endeavour to answer the third query— " What impelled the ancient Egyptians to come to Britain ? " Professor G. Elliot Smith is of opinion that the needs of the Egyptian embalmer impelled men to make voyages to obtain

the necessary resins, balsams and spices. But to seek these the ancient Egyptian would turn his eyes to the East rather than to the West, and it is to the West that we must look for an answer to our question.

The religion of ancient Egypt was in essence a Cult of the Dead. We all know of the profusion of gold found in Egyptian tombs, but few of us perhaps have ever stopped to inquire why so much gold was put there. We esteem gold largely for its exchange value. A piece of gold (once familiar to us as the sovereign, but now represented by the pound note) is of value to us because we can exchange it for so many pounds of meat, so many collars, or so many pairs of silk stockings. That is, gold is precious to us because it has an exchange value. Again, we value gold for the opportunity it gives of display : hence the gold brooch, ear-rings and chain of a generation ago, and the gilded restaurant and gilded cinema hall to-day.

Gold, to have an exchange value, must be capable of being passed from hand to hand : to have a display value it must be seen. But the ancient Egyptians buried gold in tombs. To them gold must have had a value other than an exchange or a display value. What could that value have been ? A religious one ? Very possibly, for religion is one of the highest impulses that move men.

48. The *Satapatha Brahmana,* one of the Hindu sacred books, makes gold a wondrous thing, a " life-giver "; aye, more than that—" fire, light and immortality "; in short, " a form of the gods themselves." An inscription found in a mine worked by the ancient Egyptians has been translated : " Gold is the body of the gods," and in one of the Egyptian sacred books we read that when Ra, the great sun-god, grew old, his flesh became gold.

The ancient Egyptians were sun-worshippers. They knew what we are only just beginning to appreciate—that sunshine was life. Gold to them was solid sunshine, the very essence of life. And now the true reason for the profusion of gold in Egyptian tombs comes upon us with a flash—it was to give life, immortality and god-ship to the loved and honoured one in the world to come. The greater the quantity of gold buried with the loved one, the greater the hope of immortality and of attainment to the status of a god. Gold was more than precious, it was sacred, holy, divine, and the Egyptian of old ransacked the whole of the then known world to find it.

49. There was gold for him near at hand between the Nile and the Red Sea, and these gold-fields are shown on the earliest extant mining map, known as the Turin papyrus and dated by competent authorities at about 1300 B.C. When he had exhausted this source he had to go farther afield, and the lure of gold brought him to Britain.

50. In the mind of ancient man pearls were in function closely allied to gold. As Professor Elliot Smith says, " The pearl was the quintessence of life-giving and prosperity-conferring powers : it was not only identical with the moon, but also was itself a particle of moon-substance which fell as dew into the gaping oyster."

51. Pliny tells the story of Cleopatra and the precious pearl which she dissolved in vinegar and then swallowed in order to impress Antony with her great wealth. If this rather impossible incident ever took place, there may be another possible explanation. Cleopatra may have swallowed the pearl in order to acquire what the pearl stood for—life and immortality, and if this be so, she is not the first woman nor the last who has taken a nasty medicine in order to be " beautiful for ever."

52. The seekers of gold and pearls were devotees of the heliolithic cult, and on the religious impulses which prompted man in his quest of gold and pearls, Dr. Rivers very appositely remarks that of the great culture movements of the world, " none stands out as more romantic and more wonderful than the journeys of those whose religious needs led them to erect such vast monuments as the pyramids of Egypt and Tahiti, the trilithons of Nukualofa and Stonehenge."

53. Having established the former sacred character of gold and pearls, we will now examine the evidence of their former occurrence in these Islands.

Tacitus writes : " Britain contains to reward the conqueror, mines of gold and silver and other metals. The sea produces pearls." Suetonius states that Julius Cæsar invaded Britain because of its wealth in pearls, and that on his return to Rome he presented a corselet of British pearls to the goddess Venus ; while according to Strabo, the exports from Britain in the early part of the first century consisted among other things of gold and silver.

The Esk and the Conway were once famous for pearls, and a Conway pearl is said to have been inserted into the Royal crown of England. The most famous of our pearl-bearing rivers is the Tay, but unfortunately, its pearls are all wanting in lustre, and the best have a pink tinge, a defect which coincides with the experience of Tacitus, who says that British pearls are " dusky and of a livid hue."

54. Coming to the question of the occurrence of gold in the British Isles, we may note that Professor D. Wilson thinks that gold was in very early times more abundant than it is now, and shows that there is good evidence of the finding of gold in Scotland in historic times.

The Wicklow Hills in East Ireland seem to have been once a great source of gold, and Professor Gowland is of opinion that the earliest of the gold ornaments discovered in the British Isles belong to the latter part of the Stone Age and were probably made from gold obtained from the Wicklow Hills. If this be so, the supply was by no means exhausted in the Bronze Age, as the number and distribution of gold lunulæ, torques, etc., amply testify.

Gold was also found in the West of England, especially in Wales, Devon and Cornwall : indeed, gold is sometimes found in the West even at the present day.

Gold was thus found on each side of St. George's Channel, and it may be that the search for gold caused the cultural drift of those primitive races, who, as Sir Arthur Keith observes, used St. George's Channel as a sort of corridor in their " trek " from the shores of the Mediterranean to northern climes.

55. Amber, jet and a few other substances seem to have had attributes similar to those of gold and pearls, but the consideration of these must be deferred to a subsequent occasion.

56. Unlike gold, which had a religious value, tin was apparently esteemed not on religious but on utilitarian grounds. The earliest metal implements and weapons were made of copper, often too soft for effective use. In practice, the flint knife kept a better cutting edge than the copper one, and until man discovered that copper could be hardened by mixing a little tin with it, his progress in the use of metals must have been slow. A mixture of copper and tin is known as bronze, and the man (or was it the men ?) who first discovered bronze stepped straight from the Age of Stone into the midst of the Age of Metals. He was one of the benefactors of the human

race. Who he was we know not. But we may rightly surmise that he was an Easterner, for the knowledge of bronze came from the East, and the early Easterner found copper near at hand. But tin, not so.

57. Philology would seem to favour the idea that tin was obtained first from India. The Greek for "tin" is κασσίτερος (cassiteros); the Sanscrit *kastira* is said to be derived from *kash*, "to shine." Because much tin is found in the islands off the coast of India, some have supposed that the "Easterners" (whoever they were) got the name of the metal from India. India may have been the original source, but the Easterner seems to have turned his face quite early towards the West. Perhaps one of his earliest western sources was Tuscany, where tin still occurs in irregular patches.

58. Tin-ore is found in other parts of Western Continental Europe, notably in Brittany, at Pyriæ near the mouth of the Loire, and at Villedur in Morbihan. But Cornwall has from time immemorial been *the* place for tin, and with reference to ancient Cornish tin-workings we find Professor Gowland writing : "In Cornwall the conditions for the production of the metal (tin) were especially favourable; the ore was undoubtedly abundant, and subterranean mining operations were not required, as it was found either at the surface of the ground, or at but little depth below it, disseminated through the old river gravels. From the fusibility of tin and the comparative ease with which the ore is reduced, the metal must have been produced in Cornwall not long after Neolithic man settled there."

59. Tin was first found in small grains (black-tin or tin-oxide) in the beds of streams and on the seashore. Within living memory Cornish miners when out of work made in some cases a fair living by "vanning." Armed with a pail and the flat Cornish shovel, the out-of-work miner would go to a sandy beach, take up in his shovel patches of sand which he knew from experience would be likely to contain black-tin, and with a peculiar motion of the shovel, difficult to describe, he would separate the sand from the black-tin. The sand he would throw away. The black-tin he would place in his pail to be sold ultimately to the tin smelter. The man himself would say he was "streaming" or "vanning," and streaming (streaming) is reminiscent of the time when his ancestors got the black-

tin from streams, for Bronze Age man did exactly the same as modern man, only he used a wooden pail and a wooden shovel. The " straemer " of a generation ago was an excellent example of what Sir Arthur Mitchell called " The Past in the Present." An old " straemer " once told me that in a lucky week he some-times·earned as much as £2—equivalent to nearly £4 in our money of to-day. But the streamer is now no more.

60. To sum up. Egyptians (or Easterners, or whatever we·please to call them) were here probably in the latter part of the Neolithic Age, seeking pearls and gold, valued on account of the religious ideas attached to them. Later they came for utilitarian purposes—to find tin to harden copper and make it into bronze.

61. The reader's attention may now be drawn to the map of England and Wales (Fig. 14) in which the Megalithic areas are dotted. It will be seen that there are no megaliths in Lincolnshire, Norfolk, Suffolk, Essex, Cambridge, Huntingdon, Bedford, Hertford, Middlesex and Surrey, just the counties destitute of metals. But we find good evidence of megaliths in Cornwall and Devonshire, South Wales and the Lake District, just the areas where metals are abundant. It *looks* as though there is some connection between megaliths and metals, but we must not generalise too soon.

Megaliths were, as we shall see, sacred things, and after what we have said regarding the holy character of gold and pearls it will not surprise us to find all these holy things, mega-liths, gold, pearls, in close conjunction. Did the pearl and metal seekers build the megaliths ? But we must proceed.

62. Continuing our examination of the map, we note that the megaliths around Whitby are accounted for by the presence of jet, Whitby jet, famous in our time as the material from which mourning ornaments were made. Jet is found in Bronze Age graves, and it thus seems to have been connected with mourning from the second millennium before·our era. But since the War, jet as an ornament of mourning has gone out of fashion, and Whitby jet is now no more. Thus capricious Fashion destroys a custom four thousand years old.

63. The conjunction of flint and megaliths admits .of a possible explanation. Machines are men's tools in this Age of Machinery, and we find the population of Britain at present most dense just where those essentials of machinery, coal and

iron, are to be found.   Similarly, in the latter part of the Stone
Age we have evidence of numerous peoples in the chalk areas,
just where flint, the essential for man's early tools, was to be
found.   Hence the abundant proofs of Neolithic man's presence
on the Upper Chalk of Dorset and Wiltshire, and hence perhaps

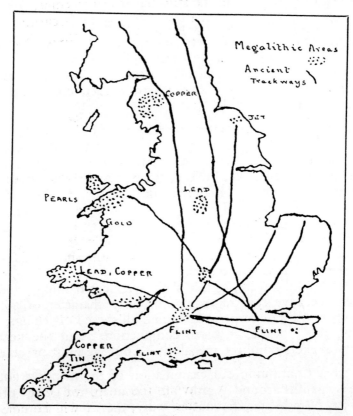

Fig. 14.
MAP. MEGALITHS AND METALS.

Avebury and Stonehenge.   The presence of flint may account
for Kits Coity House (Fig. 15), the chief megalith preserved in
Eastern and South-eastern England.

64. Copper and lead account for the megaliths found in
South Wales and the Lake and Peak Districts, while the presence
of tin seems the cause of the menhirs, cromlechs and circles
in Cornwall and Devon.   The quest of gold and pearls gives

a clue to the presence of megaliths in North Wales and in Anglesey.

65. The hæmatite of the Northampton Iron Sands was once used as a colouring matter. " The blood is the life," and corpses were once coloured red to give blood, life and strength to the beloved one in the world to come. Perhaps we may be able to return in a later essay to the fascinating questions of jet, hæmatite, amber, shells, white stones, etc., found in prehistoric graves.

W. Dexter.

Fig. 15.
KITS COITY HOUSE, KENT.

66. Before finally leaving the map, we may study the directions of the ancient trackways, and it will be noted that, generally speaking, the trackways seem to run through or near the metal-megalithic areas : also, that the trackways appear to radiate from two centres—the London and the Stonehenge areas. Stonehenge may be regarded as the Rome or Canterbury of prehistoric times, and London appears to have been a trading centre from time immemorial. Dr. Rendel Harris has shown the probability that the *Watling* in Watling Street is of Egyptian origin, and has pointed out that this prehistoric way may have been constructed by the Egyptians. What if many more of these ancient tracks are of Egyptian origin ?

67. The phrase "mines and megaliths," sometimes used instead of "metals and megaliths," is not, strictly speaking, correct, as there was very little mining (as we understand the term) in prehistoric times. Early man found gold and tin as alluvial deposits : other metals he quarried rather than mined. Still the phrase, helped as it is by " apt alliteration's artful aid," may be allowed to stand.

The hypothesis of the conjunction of mines and megaliths holds not only for England and Wales, but also for other parts of the world. Space forbids us to deal with more than two— India and Mexico. Major Munn, Inspector of Mines to the Nizam of Hyderabad, says that cromlechs are thickest in the Deccan just where the country is riddled with old workings for gold, copper and iron. In Mexico, according to Dr. W. J. Perry, archaic ruins are plentiful near the railway lines. The same motive led men of the archaic civilisation to build cities in these spots as caused modern engineers to construct the railways, and that motive was the lure of metals.

68. The following remarks seem to give general support to the theory of the conjunction of mines and megaliths. Monsieur de Morgan points out that the distribution of cromlechs is explained by their association with ancient gold and copper mines. Professor Gordon Childe writes : " It is no accident that the oldest and most numerous western megaliths cluster around the south coasts of Brittany and the Channel Islands; for it is just here that early voyagers travelling to the goldfields of Ireland and the amber coasts of Denmark would be most likely to call, and gold was once found in Brittany too." And again : " Megalithic tombs are often found in regions rich in tin and copper (Sardinia, Portugal, the Cevennes, Cornwall); or gold (Portugal, Brittany, Ireland); or silver (Spain, Sardinia); or amber (Denmark). But the coincidence between the distribution of megaliths and metals is by no means exact," which is only a way of saying that there is an exception to every rule.

69. Dr. W. J. Perry has made this subject especially his own, and has shown that megalithic monuments cluster thickest in and around those regions which produced gold, copper, tin, amber and pearls, especially if those regions were near the sea, or on ancient trade routes. Professor G. Elliot Smith admirably sums up when he says that the theory " Metals— Megaliths " not only holds for England and Wales, but seems

to apply " to the whole world with the possible exception of Australia."

The theory has, however, been hotly contested—as all new theories are—by the majority of archæologists, but on the whole it seems to hold its ground.

70. Our stone circles are believed to have been erected by sun-worshippers, our cromlechs by those who practised the cult of the dead, and both circle and cromlech seem to have been built by metal-seekers. Sun-worship, cult of dead, metal-seeking, all point to the East, and preferably to Egypt, but the claims of Mesopotamia and of the Eastern Mediterranean must not be forgotten.

71. Mines and megaliths ! Mines and megaliths ! ! There they have been side by side for 3000–4000 years, yet it was not till this generation that the conjunction was noticed. Really, we are not half so observant, half so clever, as we sometimes think we are !

72. But to return to our subject. It is hoped that the reader now considers the following facts fairly well established : (1) That Britain once had a fair abundance of pearls and gold, and (2) that the possession of these sacred treasures impelled the ancient Egyptians and other Easterners to seek our shores, perhaps as early as the third millennium before our era.

73. We have now the task of demonstrating that these Easterners may have introduced some of their civilisation here. Objections we have to meet are that they could have come only in boat-loads, that their sojourn here was but a brief one, and that they could not possibly have affected the ancient inhabitants of these islands to any appreciable extent.

74. Our answer is that these Easterners were most probably colonists here, not transient visitors, and accordingly, their influence upon the aborigines must have been profound. Professor Fleure in his investigations on the physical characteristics of the Welsh found " dark, stalwart, broad-headed men on certain coastal patches, often curiously associated with megaliths in Wales." These men differ from the Welsh, and similar types have been found about Wicklow in Ireland (once famous for its gold), in Cornwall (still noted for its tin) and elsewhere. Professor Fleure is of opinion that these dark broad-headed people have some of the blood of the people who built the

megaliths. The people who built these megalithic monuments were not here to-day and gone to-morrow. They had permanent trading stations and colonies in these Islands, and they formed alliances, matrimonial or otherwise, with the natives.

75. As Professor Elliot Smith observes : " New customs and beliefs were *not* adopted at most of the places where the ancient mariners must have touched in their voyages. It was only in those localities where gold mines or pearl beds caused them to tarry and compel the local population to work for them in exploiting these new sources of wealth that the new knowledge took root. It was only when the more cultured aliens dominated the aborigines and forced them to do the things that they (the immigrant minority) wanted done that these things were done. . . . Reason plays a surprisingly small part in such advances, except on the part of the real pioneers ; for the herd, it is either actual compulsion or moral suasion . . . that brings about the change. . . . In most cases only actual compulsion can effect such advancement."

76. Our civilisation has had great effect (for good or ill) upon subject races of a low degree of culture such as are to be found in Southern Africa and India ; its effect upon such a country as China has been all but negligible. According to Dr. Rivers, " The more developed and highly organised the culture of a country, the less is the effect upon it of our own people. In such a country as China the effect of European influence has been slow and in amount is still very slight. . . . In India again, it is doubtful whether, except in material culture, our influence has really been much greater. We have had little effect on social structure, on the caste system, on language or on religion, and it is noteworthy that the greatest effect has been in those parts of India where the indigenous culture has remained at a relatively low level. It is only in the south that the English language and the Christian religion have obtained any hold on the people."

77. It has been said that the last glacial epoch had hardly passed away in Britain before evidence is found of foreign adventurers and traders on our shores. The aborigines of Britain, whoever they were, had had no time to develop ; their culture was necessarily low, and it easily fell before the infinitely superior culture from the East.

78. In Cornwall the dark, broad-headed people referred to in a previous paragraph are popularly supposed to be the descendants of sailors wrecked in the Spanish Armada. I have written " popularly " : I ought rather to have written " generally." A university man once told me that this idea of Spanish descent muſt be true—the faƈt was recorded in Mr. So-and-So's Family Bible! We know fairly well where moſt of the ships of the Armada were wrecked : many of them off the north-weſt coaſt of Scotland. There is no record whatever of even one ship of the Armada having been wrecked off the coaſt of Cornwall. Dr. Rendel Harris in his essays has shown that the ancient Egyptians were great colonisers, and he has gone so far as to indicate very possible sites of ancient Egyptian colonies in Britain. These Cornish " Spaniards " have some of the blood of Eaſtern (perhaps Egyptian) coloniſts, and if these Cornish " Spaniards " had kept their pedigrees, they could proudly boaſt of an anceſtry not as recent as A.D. 1588, but as far back as 1588 B.C.

79. Still, we cannot yet ſtate as an absolute faƈt that the Egyptians were coloniſts here, although the presumption is exceedingly ſtrong, and so we have to meet the challenge that a boat-load of people could not have influenced a whole hoſt of aborigines. The answer is far easier than at firſt sight appears. Professor Elliot Smith observes, " I would like to remind those who maintain that small groups of men cannot effeƈt any influence in a foreign land what Pizarro accomplished in 1532. With a mere handful of men he dominated the vaſt powers of the Incas. . . . There is no reason why these earlier adventurers (*the Prospeƈtors or the Children of the Sun*) should not have dealt with the Americans (or indeed with any other natives) of their day in much the same way as Pizarro did."

Other inſtances may be given. About 1804 twenty-seven convicts escaped from New South Wales to the Fijian Islands, where they acquired great influence largely due to their fire-arms, and if they had been more worthy representatives of their race, their influence might have been greater ſtill.

The ſtory of Sir James Brooke reads more like a mediæval romance than a piece of nineteenth-century hiſtory. He is euphemiſtically said to have been " imbued with the spirit of the old adventurers of Elizabethan times." In reality, he was a gentleman in search of adventure in the Southern Seas Backed by the crew of one small brig, he landed at Sarawak, Borneo, in 1839, and speedily got himself acclaimed Rajah and Governor of Sarawak, a kingly position held by his descendants to this day.

80. Big brains backed by a modicum of force will generally win their way among peoples possessed of more force but less brains. Most of our really good things came from the East, and there is nothing wildly improbable in supposing the possibility of "a boat-load" of ancient metal-seekers or Easterners dominating the aborigines and introducing their civilisation among them. The hypothesis that the first civilisation in these Islands was introduced by Eastern metal-seekers is not to be dismissed with a superior sneer. Time will show that there is " more in it " than some of us at present will admit.

81. To sum up. We may consider it as proved that the Ancient Britons who opposed the Roman Invasions were civilised and not the barbarians they are generally considered to have been. Further, we may agree that a strong presumption has been established that there was a civilisation here (archaic, not modern; intrusive, not indigenous) perhaps as early as 2000 B.C.

Just think of the prospect which this idea calls up. Leaving out of consideration sundry lacunæ of darkness, doubt and uncertainty, we have a fairly continuous history of Britain for nearly 2000 years—from the first invasion of Cæsar to the present day.

But there is another history of 2000 years' duration from the end of the Stone Age to the first Roman Invasion—in other words, there is as much history of Britain to learn as we already know. Here and there we get a fact or two, a glimpse or two of light. We are like little children who try to put together a jig-saw puzzle of which most of the pieces are missing. But more and more pieces are being discovered every day, and although we can never expect to find them all, yet we may dare to hope to find so many as to be in a position to make a reasonable inference regarding the nature of the whole picture. Perchance before the next century is far advanced the history of Britain will be commenced, not at 55 B.C., the date of the Invasion of Julius Cæsar, but at about 2000 B.C., the approximate date of the erection of Avebury.

BOOKS RECOMMENDED FOR READING

Suitable for beginners in the subject :—

†A. MACKENZIE, D.
   * (a) *Ancient Man in Britain.* Blackie, 1922.
   * (b) *Ancient Civilisations.* Blackie, 1927.

Suitable for more advanced students :—

B. ELLIOT SMITH, G.
   * (a) *Rock-cut Tomb and Dolmen,* 1913.
   (b) *Migrations of Early Culture,* 1915.
   (c) *Primitive Man,* 1916.
   * (d) *Ships as evidences of Migrations of Early Culture,* 1917.
   * (e) *Ancient Egypt,* 1923.
   (f) *Evolution of the Dragon.*

C. PERRY, W. J.
   * (a) *Megaliths and Mines.* Proc. Manchester Lit. & Phil. Soc.,
      Vols. 60 (1915) and 65 (1920–21).
   * (b) *Children of the Sun,* 1924.
   (c) *Growth of Civilisation,* 1924.

D. RIVERS, W. H. R.
   Psychology and Ethnology, 1926.

E. HARRIS, RENDEL.
   Woodbrooke Essays. Heffer & Co., Cambridge.
   (a) No. 1. *Traces of Ancient Egypt in Mediterranean.*
   (b) No. 6. *More about Egypt and its Colonies.*
   (c) No. 11. *Egypt in Britain.*
   (d) No. 17. *Watling St.*
   (e) No. 18. *Watendlath.*

F. CHILDE, V. GORDON. Kegan Paul, Trench, Trübner & Co.
   * (a) *Dawn of European Civilisation,* 1925.
   * (b) *The Aryans,* 1926.
   (c) *The Most Ancient East,* 1928.

G. PEAKE, H.
   *   Bronze Age and Celtic World,* 1922.

H. PEET, T. E.
   *   Rough Stone Monuments,* 1912.

I. WILSON, D.
   Prehistoric Annals of Scotland, 1863.

J. BRITISH MUSEUM GUIDES.
   (a) *Stone Age.* * (b) *Bronze Age.* (c) *Iron Age.*

K. GOWLAND, W.
   *   Metals in Antiquity,* 1912.

† These letters A(a), B(a), etc., are used to denote Books in " References " given on next page.
* Books specially recommended.

37

REFERENCES

SECTION.

9. Against this view, Sir A. Keith in *Times*, January, 1929.
12. Evans, John. *Coins of Ancient Britons*, 1864; *Supplement*, 1890.
13. *J, (b), Index sub Enamels : Plates I, VIII, etc. Philostratus. Iconium I, XXVIII, q. Soc. Ant. Scot., XIX, 49. F, (a), 299, 301.
14. *Antiq. Journ.*, VI, No. 2, p. 177, Plate XXIX. *Brit. Acad.*, II (1906), 185–217.
15. Diodorus Siculus, v. 22. *Bel. Gal.*, VI, 14.
17. J, (c), Index sub Mirrors. *R. Inst. Corn.* III (1868–70), 34–48, with two plates. Borlase, W. C., Naenia Cornubia (1872), 246. J, (b), 93, plate VII and fig. 98. J, (b), Index sub Lunettes and fig. 93 : also sub Torcs and fig. 44.
18. *Archæologia*, LVIII (1903), 37–118.
19. Wheeler, R. E. M., *Prehist. and Roman Wales*, 281.
20. Allcroft, A. H., *Earthworks of England* (1908). R. C. Hoare, *Anc. Wilts.*, 113, 170. *Antiquity*, I, 90, 99. *Prehistorische Zeitschrift*, XV, 32.
26. Leslie Forbes, *Early Races of Scotland* (1866), I, 185.
23. Leeds, E. T., in *Archæologia*, LXXX.
29. D, 147, 148. Gomme, G. L., *Ethnology in Folk Lore* (1892), 165. Bertrand, A., *La Religion des Gaulois* (1897), I. 3.
32. D, 250–256. B, (a). J, (a), 131. *Man*, XIII, 105. Seligman, C. G., *Brit. Assn.*, 1915.
34. *L'Anthropologie*, XXX (1921), 235. *Quest. des Chron. et d'Ethnog.* (1913), 33.
35. F, (c), Ch. IX. H, 147, 148.
36. B, (d), passim; Budge, Wallis, *The Mummy* (1925), 30, 31. Erman, A., *Anc. Egypt* (1894), 508–513.
37. Erman, A., *Anc. Egypt* (1894), 482, 489; A, (b), 91.
38. *Soc. Antiq. Scot.*, I, 44, 45; XI, 148–151.
39. *Bel. Gal.* III, 13–15. Cambray, J. de, *Monuments Celtiques* (1805), 172.
40. *Times*, 10th Oct., 1928.
41. Sayce, A. H., *Reminiscences*, 405. Evans, Arthur, *Palace of Minos*, 1, 491, 492, 493.
43. Rhys. J., *Celtic Folk Lore* (1901), II, 681, 665, q. Johnson, W., *Folk Memory* (1908), 86.
45. Budge, Wallis, *Egypt. Hierog.*, 191 sub uten.
46. E, (a), (b), (c), (d), (e).
47. B, (f).
48. A, (a), 80. Erman, A., *Anc. Egypt*, 467, q. Lepsius' *Denkmäler aus Aegypten und Aethiopien*, iii, 140c.
49. Chabas, *Inscrip. des Mines d'Or* (1862), 30–36, q. *Agricola* (1912), 129, n. 16. Alford, *Rep. on Gold Mining in Egypt*, 1900.
50. B, (f), 99, 156.
51. Pliny, *Nat. Hist.*, IX, 58.
52. Rivers, (a), 256.

* For meanings of these letters see " Books recommended for Reading."

53. Tacitus, *Agricola*, XII. Suetonius, *Julius*, XLVI. Pliny, *Nat. Hist.*, IX, 57. Watkins, M. G., *Nat. Hist. of Ancients* (1885), 254, 255. Martin Martin, *West. Isles* (Edn. 1884), 141, 142. Macfarlane, *Geog. Coll.* (1906–8), I, 92, 203; III, 212, 252. Tacitus, *Agricola*, XII.

54. I. Vol. I, 322.
   K. (25), 259. R. *Inst. Corn.*, I, No. 3, *Supp.* p. 34; XII, 56; XIII, 131; XVI, 103. *Times*, 10 Oct., 1928.

57. I. Vol. I, 305.

58. K, (17), 251; (14), 248. *Agricola*, Edn. 1912, p. 411, note 53.

65. *Paviland Cave* by W. J. Sollas, Royal Anthrop. Soc. (1913).

67. Munn, L., *Manchester Lit. & Phil. Soc.*, No. 54 (1921), C, (b), 66.

68. de Morgan, *Les Premiers Civil.* (1909), 404. F, (a), 274, 131.

69. C, (a), Vol. LX, 16; Vol. LXV, No. 13. H, passim. Corkill, W. H., *Manx Mines* in *Manchester Lit. & Phil. Soc.*, XLV (1920–1), No. 7. Elliot Smith in Intro. to Jackson's *Shells* (1917), XXIII. F, (b), 292.

71. F, (c), 140 etc.

74. Fleure, H. J., in R. *Anthrop. Soc.*, XLV (1916), 137, 138, and in *Human Geog. in W. Europe* (1918), 16, but see F, (a), 284.

75. B, (d), 20.

76. D, 300, 301.

78. E, (a), (b), (c), (e).

79. B, (d), 10, 11. Williams, T., *Fiji* (1858), 3. St. John's *Life of Sir James Brooke.*